WINNING
IN BUSINESS WITH
ADHD

WINNING
IN BUSINESS WITH
ADHD

13 RULES TO MAKE ADHD
WORK FOR YOU

HADAR Y. SWERSKY

CREATIVE GEEKS

Published by. Creative Geeks Press

For speaking engagements or general inquiries:
speaking@winninginbusinesswithadhd.com

winninginbusinesswithadhd.com

ISBN 978-1-7371047-0-4 (paperback)
ISBN 978-1-7371047-1-1 (eBook)

FIRST EDITION

—

Editor: James Gallagher

Illustrator: Walker Howard

Publisher & Book Designer: Kory Kirby
SET IN SABON LT PRO

Contents

"*ADHD is like having a Ferrari engine for a brain with bicycle brakes. Strengthen the brakes and you have a champion.*"

— DR. EDWARD HALLOWELL, *former faculty member of the Harvard Medical School*

TLDR: Too Long; Didn't Read

1. This book is about business, but it can help you with other areas of your life.
2. The book provides a set of basic rules I have used to succeed. Don't dismiss the book if one idea does not work for you.
3. Each rule has a TLDR, followed by a more detailed description. The TLDR will summarize each rule in as few words as possible, and you can get the point without reading the longer description.
4. The book does not provide a formula for success, but it is an eye-opener. You are smart. After reading this book, you can create your own follow-up rules.

Introduction

You might be wondering why this book is so short. But if it were longer, would you actually read it?

We both know the answer to this question. This book is aimed at people who don't have the patience to read. It is aimed at readers who "get it" immediately and lose patience when people repeat themselves or state the obvious.

You have ADHD, or at least you think you do. You are extremely talented. You have done well (and perhaps have thrown it all away once or twice). You are impossible to live with but are **full of charm** (as a doctor once told me, people with ADHD are super charming; otherwise they would all be murdered by the age of seventeen).

But you feel you can do better, or you wouldn't have picked up this book (no, not you, Mom). So allow me to take just a few minutes of your time.

This is my form of a journal. The book documents my journey through all the following:

- Realizations.
- Learning from mistakes.
- Coming to terms with my internal challenges.
- Putting ADHD to work for me.

This is a work in progress, just like life and I can barely bring myself to "wrap it up" and say these are the rules! But I must. Otherwise this book will stay on my hard drive and I won't achieve the goal I was aiming for when I started writing it.

My Story

Most people say I am a successful businessperson: versatile, unintimidated, quick, sharp-tongued and at times too direct. It is that last point I always have an issue with. In my eyes I have a heart of gold. I never mean harm or, God forbid, to offend anyone! For years I did not understand how what was going on inside my head could be so different from what the outside world sees or hears.

When I "preach" a point aggressively, I am doing so passionately because I care about the person in front of me. When I say to a friend, "I think you could have done better," I actually mean to say, "I believe you are amazing. Why are you settling for so little?"

And while everyone was praising my success, I was beating myself up for not being able to capitalize more from an opportunity.

I could probably go on for hours, but all this changed when I was about thirty-seven years old. I have four kids, and just before my first daughter approached her fifth birthday, I went to be diagnosed for ADHD—an eye-opener! Since then my life has never been the same.

It was an eye opener, suddenly **everything** made sense! I was walking around mesmerized.

I then realized that after living with ADHD (yes, I have the *H* big-time!) for so many years without knowing I had it, I developed unconventional methods for dealing with my "flaws" (yes, they are not flaws, but that is how I saw them). From that point on, I started looking around and realized a few things:

- Most of my friends have ADD or ADHD.
- They have all developed amazing methods to conquer challenges that come with this condition.

I also realized that many of them lacked a clear understanding of their position, their challenges and the basic tools to tackle these challenges. So I set off to write this book—thank you, **medication!**

The first thing I realized was that if you don't have ADHD, you simply cannot "get it." I compare it to sex (corny but useful). You can tell people about it. You can show them videos and describe it for hours on hours. But you can "get it" only when you "do it." Or in the case of ADHD, once you "have it."

As an international entrepreneur, I travel almost every other week. I get to meet dozens of people in various countries and settings. Once I "got it" that I "have it" and learned to recognize ADHD in its many forms, I started to discover that all over the world amazing people were tackling ADHD in unique and exciting ways, and there is SO much to learn from them.

I decided to embark on a journey where I would ask the questions and identify methods that can help me or benefit others. I wanted to simplify these methods, or as we like to say at my company, *dumbify* them so they are easy to remember and simple to follow.

The big challenge for my readers is to read the book cover to cover, so I have made it ADHD friendly. You can browse through the topics and just read the TLDRs. Or you can bite the bullet—or take Ritalin, Adderall, or any other pill you choose—and *actually* read all the words I wrote.

Happy browsing!
☺

Basic Rules (Start Here)

This book does not cover every possible obstacle or situation. It is merely a humble starting point based on my personal experiences, and it should provide building blocks for creating your bespoke day-to-day reality. While some rules may not apply to you or your business methods, they should all provide food for thought that you can adapt for your own use.

#1

Get Diagnosed

TLDR

You think you have ADHD. You *know* you have ADHD. Whatever. Get diagnosed. It isn't just so you know you have it—it's to help you *get to know yourself.* You will be surprised when you read what the diagnosis says. If you went for a proper diagnosis, it isn't a simple yes or no. It will help you understand who you are and understand that your challenges are not only yours. They are shared by millions.

DESCRIPTION

For years I "knew" I had ADHD. But without any official recognition, I couldn't get myself to embark on this journey and understand it.

About five years before I was diagnosed, I learned something surprising. When I was fifteen or sixteen, I was sent to a psychologist who diagnosed my ADHD, but my parents decided not to "share" the results with me so I didn't feel that I have a "handicap." (I remember going, but I never got the feedback.)

Without criticizing my wonderful parents, who did what they thought best, this was a mistake. Through my military service and studies, not to mention my work career, I have encountered dozens of situations that would have been much easier to handle had I known of my "condition" or challenges.

#2

Remove Your Distractions

TLDR

You cannot do more than one thing at a time, at least not properly. If you are writing emails, put your phone on silent. If you go into meetings, go without a mobile phone, and so on. You get the point.

DESCRIPTION

This is so simple to follow that there isn't much to say about it. I never attend meetings with a mobile phone. If you have meetings in your office, don't have them with a screen in front of you. You might think you are just glancing at the screen, but you are being distracted and not concentrating on what is being said. Furthermore, we both know that if you get a message that invokes serious emotion, such as happiness or anger, the meeting you are in is as good as done, because you will not be able to focus. It is rude, and it makes meetings last longer than needed, which is a waste of time.

#3

Control Your Temper

TLDR

You are impatient. This leads to frustration and anger.
Watch what you say. You cannot take it back.

DESCRIPTION

While this seems easy, and may be obvious, your temper tends to come from impatience. Most people are not as quick as you. But they are there for a reason, and they are probably more methodical than you and can complete the task fully, albeit a bit slower. Don't be hard on yourself. A short temper is an ADHD trait. Learn to acknowledge it and then accept it.

#4

Write Things Down

TLDR

Get organized and write things down. No, you will NOT remember it in five minutes . . .

Create a system, but don't overcomplicate it or try to achieve too many things at once. This is so you can actually follow through and succeed as opposed to trying to "overdo it"—and ending up not doing it at all.

Furthermore, people with ADHD tend to make declarations such as "from now on I will never. . ." which sets them up for failure. Take baby steps, not "life changing decisions." Think of it as something you need to do for one day, and take it one day at a time. If you decide you are going to change from now to whenever, you will probably fail, as the task would be too daunting without any small successes along the way.

DESCRIPTION

While this sounds simple, it is not easy to continuously commit to this. First, stop trusting your memory. While it is probably sharp, you also probably drop things that seem trivial or make you uncomfortable (like paying a traffic fine). These matters tend to come back and bite you.

Things that you can complete in minutes are often delayed for months. Once you realize this, create a system for writing down (in any way you feel comfortable) all the things you need to do. Then set reminders. Don't trust yourself to come back to the list, because chances are you won't.

Use calendar reminders or simple to-do lists. Once you have created your system, it will be easier to complete all your tasks.

This has an additional health benefit, of dropping your anxiety level, because you know everything will be taken care of. Most important, you won't forget anything.

#5

Stop Talking, Start Listening

TLDR

Listen, don't talk. It is simple, yet so difficult!

DESCRIPTION

Don't go into a room and start talking. That isn't why you walked into the room. Sit down and listen. Ask what they think and in the end tell them your opinion. Otherwise, all you are going to hear is what *they think* you just said and not what they think.

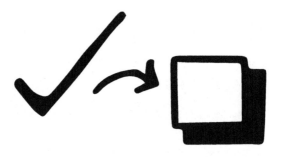

#6

Almost Done Is Not Done! There Is an Order to Getting Things Done

TLDR

Finish tasks. Yes, it is almost done. Just a little bit left to do. Do it and get it over with. Focus on finishing tasks until there is **nothing left to be done**, not even a simple two-second task. Get it done! *Capisce?*

DESCRIPTION

Set a list of priorities and then follow it. Get it done. Not later. Not after I do this little fun thing first or this other thing that is so much more interesting. Just do it! Getting stuff out of the way is fun and is extremely productive.

People who do not have ADHD simply do things. As ADHD is genetic, you probably learned at home to postpone stuff that you don't feel like doing. In some cases, these things might be delayed perpetually.

A great secret to getting things done is doing them. Yes, this might seem obvious, but it's a good thing to remember. And once it is done, it is done! No more need to remember. No more excuses for why it wasn't done. No late fees and a host of issues you have probably come to know intimately.

There are no shortcuts. There is no quick way of getting things done. Just get them done properly without cutting any corners. You will quickly find that you have **so much more time,** because you are not constantly returning to do tasks that you could have already finished.

Prioritize, and then work according to the priorities you have set. This sounds simple, but is one of the hardest things to do when you have ADHD. Working according to an order that isn't the "what I feel like doing" order is difficult for us. But it is necessary and yields great results.

#7

The George Clooney Rule

TLDR

Focus, focus and then **FOCUS!** Choose one idea, sleep on it, research it and then go for it. Don't hedge your bets. Business is about failing. Don't be scared of it. It will get difficult. You will encounter obstacles, but the grass is not greener in the next business idea. **Find your passion and stick with it!** Sticking to your goals is hard enough. Passion helps you stay on course.

You'll need to read (or skip) to the end of this rule to learn how this rule got its name . . .

DESCRIPTION

"Success is not final, failure is not fatal: it is the courage to continue that counts."

— *Winston Churchill*

We've all heard the stories. We all know a guy who stumbled upon an idea and made millions without any hard work. Unfortunately, while these people do exist, they are few and far between. Most successful people try many times before they hit that one thing that makes them successful. There are no shortcuts, just a lot of hard work and getting up after you get beaten down.

You also cannot efficiently do many things at the same time or expect to do them properly. While you might think that you are hedging your bets by doing a couple of things at the same time, what happens is that you are only doing a couple of things *partially*, instead of one thing *properly*.

A young entrepreneur once came to me for advice. This guy was working twenty hours a day. He was doing okay but constantly jumping from one thing to another, be it business introductions or importation of goods. When I asked him why he was doing so many things at the same time, he said he didn't know which one would work, so he ran in multiple directions until something hit.

But even when something hit, he didn't let the other things go because he thought they had potential. I asked him to imagine what would have been the result of focusing on one thing, and we chose an example of one of his businesses: if he had invested all his efforts in this business for the past six months, he would have been more successful (and less stressed).

I also highlighted that driving his multifocus abilities at one business would have resulted in him finding new ways to push his business in the right direction, developing it and increasing his chances of success.

Focus also gives you the ability to truly understand a niche. It allows you to build expertise in your chosen area and become an expert. This will develop into a huge advantage, because you will reach the 10,000-hour goal and combine this knowledge with your creativity to propel your business to the next level. If you are not familiar with the 10,000 hours concept, Google it. It might be controversial, yet one can still learn a lot from this concept.

Yes, you are very talented. You can do anything, but if you don't **love it,** you won't stick to it—and this becomes much more difficult when you have ADHD.

Staying on track is much easier when you love what you do. Every business has challenges, and you succeed by continuing to "apply consistent pressure" when things get hard or don't go your way.

George Clooney is a great example. The Hollywood megastar was a broke actor who only made it in his thirties when he got his big chance in the hit series *ER*. Few people know he was a waiter who was basically working just to pay his rent. But he kept focusing on his target and following his passion. He believed he would eventually succeed and pursued his dream until he made it, while not getting distracted. Inspiring!

I WILL BE THERE
IN 5 MINUTES!

#8

Being Late and
Making Promises

TLDR

Stop being late and making promises you cannot realistically keep. It is annoying and disrespectful.

DESCRIPTION

Nothing takes two minutes. No, you cannot do just one more thing before you leave. While these promises are coming from a good place within your heart, they are causing heartache to those who are waiting to get a work document from you that you did not deliver on time, or at all. Yes, it was just another two minutes to finish, but you never sent it . . . As my good friend says, "Arriving on time is the equivalent of being late."

#9

Beware of Employing People with ADHD

TLDR

They are fun and you are drawn to them, but they might **not be what you really need**. Don't succumb to the "fun" of hiring people with ADHD. Evaluate the work required and try to think of who you would like to complete this task. Would it work better with a person with ADHD or not?

I see employees with ADHD like super high-tech rockets that require significant support staff to achieve lift off. Seeing as you started the business, or are running it, there is already enough fire power and you should surround yourself with people who are strong where you are weak. Of course once your business grows you will need more rockets, but by now you know to recognize them and the positions you need them to fill and will be able to evaluate accordingly.

DESCRIPTION

So many times I have found myself drawn to hiring people with ADHD. Actually, why not? We are fun, exciting, diverse, unexpected. True . . . but that doesn't help us achieve our business tasks and goals. Isn't it enough that most of your friends have ADHD? (If you haven't noticed, look again.)

I remember the first time I took Ritalin. It was **boring**. I thought: "Is this how the other side lives?" I seriously wanted to kill myself. It was terrible. But after years of watching people who don't have ADHD, I noticed they don't feel like that. It is simply their reality, and you can use their ability to perform repetitive, mundane tasks to your advantage.

Simply find smart, organized people with a passion to succeed and show them the way. Then let them perform these tasks that would cost you time and sanity . . . and let's be honest, you probably won't **ever** do these task anyway.

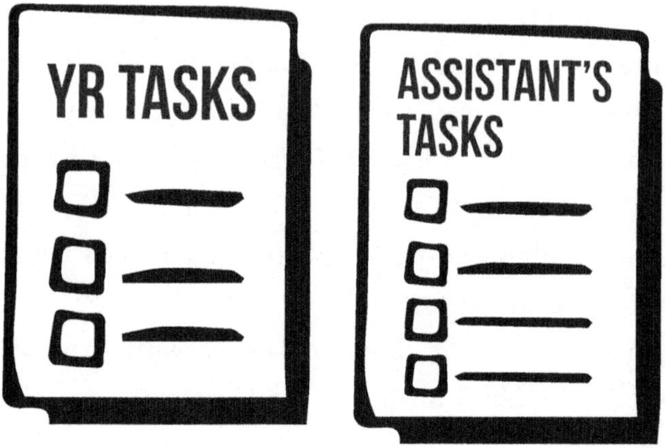
YR TASKS
ASSISTANT'S TASKS

#10

Yes, You Can Do It. But Should You? Get an Assistant or Two!

TLDR

Repetitive or mundane tasks take a huge toll, whether you recognize it or not. Get an assistant. Put in place systems and processes that the assistant can easily follow and invest the time in training them. This will free your mind to deal with tasks only you can handle!

DESCRIPTION

Yes, you can take care of it. But you won't, not until the last minute, if ever. This situation will create pressure and will stress out everyone around you. Invest the time in showing someone how to do a task, and enjoy watching it happen while you have time to let your mind roam.

You will come to appreciate stuff being done, systems put in place and ongoing monitoring. While this isn't an easy financial decision to take, it is a game changer.

#11

Stop Changing Your Mind—It's Infuriating!

TLDR

You are a leader (or you want to be) and your staff need clear guidance! They need simple tasks and goals to follow. That is why they need you. Make up your mind, decide on a course of action, lay out the steps and then describe them. Communication is key, so communicate these steps, move aside, and let stuff happen.

DESCRIPTION

We are great at starting things, but we hardly ever complete them. I can show you hundreds of projects I started and never finished. The secret is finishing projects, and for that you need to define a clear end goal. As someone once said to me, the only thing better than "perfect" is "done."

If it is writing a book, then the process is easy to define. But if the goal is to start a company or a new venture, then there is no real end. For that I would recommend setting interim goals that ensure you are making progress.

When you start off with a project, set out the stepping stones. These are the stages of a project, and you'll want to keep your eye on the next stepping stone. While people with ADHD tend to try to complete multiple tasks in parallel, this should be limited to tasks that help you achieve your next stepping stone. You would be astounded at how many things can be achieved and at how efficient you will be. I believe this will then be followed by an overwhelming sense of relief for getting stuff done.

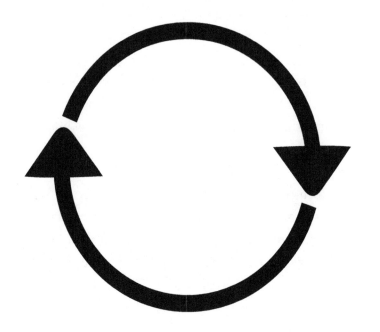

#12

Now Start from the Beginning

TLDR

Don't skim through emails. When you reach the end, it is time to start reading it properly, without emotions.

DESCRIPTION

Oh so many times we get long emails. We scan them, reach a conclusion and react, but we never really read them. A trick I was once taught is to write at the end, "Well now, Mr. or Mrs. ADHD, it is time you read this email properly, so please start again from the beginning."

It actually works. It's astonishing how many times I have used this phrase at the end of a long email and gotten a reply such as, "That was so accurate!" We cannot teach everyone how to be better at their job, but since you are reading this book, I encourage you to read it again once you are done skimming through it.

Seriously, I know that's a lot to ask, but you will be surprised how much you missed or misunderstood since you were overwhelmed with emotions while reading.

#13

The Most
Important Rule

TLDR

This is by far my golden rule, so pay attention. No short-cuts here!

DESCRIPTION

Never decide on the spot. Always wait one day before making big decisions. This rule has saved me from making huge mistakes. Because I have ADHD, I tend to be impulsive, so I do not make any decisions on the spot. This helps me avoid situations where my enthusiasm gets the better of me. It prevents me from committing to something I can't follow through on or committing to something that seems foolish the next day.

Give yourself at least one day. You will be surprised what comes out.

Got it? Now read this short bit again, because this is my number one rule. (And if you jumped to the end and started with this rule, then **gotcha!**) Now start from the beginning. That is why I have TLDRs, so you can finish this book in less than five minutes.

Final Words

You did it! You reached the end of my book! Take a moment and congratulate yourself, you have taken a small, yet huge step forward.

I hope you enjoyed this book on the basic rules I have used to succeed. I also like to think of these rules as processes. The more I have learned to respect these processes, the more impactful each process was to my businesses, and my life.

This book took a small effort to write and a huge effort to finish. I hope you make the most of it.

I would love to read your feedback and hear more about your personal experiences!

reader@winninginbusinesswithADHD.com
winninginbusinesswithadhd.com

About the Author

Hadar Y. Swersky is a serial entrepreneur, keynote speaker and author of *Winning in Business with ADHD* which is his private "ADHD in business" playbook. This easy to read book describes his basic rules, the reasoning behind them and provides the reader with actionable insights that will immediately improve their business skills.

Printed in Great Britain
by Amazon